NAVY
BLUE

BUD HUNTON

To order additional copies of this book, contact:
Xlibris
1-888-795-4274
www.Xlibris.com
Orders@Xlibris.com

ISBN: Softcover   978-1-7960-7524-3
         Hardcover   978-1-7960-7525-0
         EBook   978-1-7960-7523-6

Print information available on the last page

Rev. date: 11/29/2019

NAVY BLUE

"Friendship is the best kind of ship"
Jennifer Lane, Streamline

PROLOGUE

At the end of my basic training in 1955, my Company Commander, Chief McGinty sat down with me for what was considered an exit interview. He opened the conversation with "so Hunton, do you want to be a Navy Blue Jacket*?" I replied "yes sir" and he then reviewed my performance during boot camp. A few weeks earlier McGinty had just been promoted to Chief and he was in a very good mood. He was the first Chief Petty Officer that I had ever met and I was inspired by his high level of confidence and authority. Throughout the past week he had been carrying a box of cigars as our company moved throughout the compound. Whenever a friend of his was nearby, McGinty offered each one a cigar and a handshake. After my exit interview, the Chief informed me that I was being assigned to Hospital Corps School and my orders were ready. My grades in high school were good, especially in biology, which would be helpful in the medical field that I was entering. Chief went on to encourage me to finish my high school education and set my sights high for the future. Years later when I was promoted to Chief Petty Officer, I would remember his words of wisdom.

Blue jacket: a seaman of a British Warship/and enlisted man in the U.S. Navy

Navy Blue will take you to many interesting places in the world, exploring historical events and unusual situations as seen through the eyes of a teenager who gradually matures into a world traveler. The journey starts at the U.S. Naval Base at Great Lakes, Illinois moving across country via train to San Francisco, California and then heading west via U.S. Airforce military transportation. The author spends the next two years in Yokosuka, Japan exploring its culture and country side such as Mt. Fuji. Leaving Japan in 1959 he will work his way back aboard his first ship the USS Dixie (AD-14), stopping in Hawaii for seven days. Once back stateside the next trip takes Bud to his birthplace of Philadelphia, where he is assigned to the U.S. Naval Hospital on South Broad Street. He will be reunited with aunts, uncles and cousins residing in North Philadelphia. Uncle Freddy, a truck driver made a living driving a beer truck. Freddy was an unforgettable character who frequently answered the front door with a bottle of beer in his hand. After leaving Philly as a trained X-ray Technologist, many new doors will open for Bud and his new wife Beverly as they travel together around the country.

On the Move-getting started

Over a twenty year period of time, we moved an average of every eighteen to twenty four months. This was a challenge to Bev and I plus our four girls, Patty, Sue, Linda and Debbie. In fact, when we were packing for our next move, we often found boxes from our last move that had not been unpacked. Changing schools was difficult for the girls and the quality of education varied from state to state. We found that some of the smaller southern communities were lacking in educational standards and we could see the difference in how our girls reacted to the various schools.

When receiving orders to various ships we resided in areas such as Norfolk and Portsmouth Virginia, Charleston, South Carolina, Jacksonville, North Carolina and Goose Creek, S.C. All of the duty stations were related to previous training as a Hospital Corpsman, independent duty specialist, and Field Medicine Tech., including an eighteen month tour in Jacksonville, North Carolina with the Marines. The U.S. Marine Corps does not have their own medics. Navy Corpsman are drafted for an eighteen to twenty four month tour of duty. Prior to reporting for their assignment, corpsman are required to take several weeks of basic training where they are orientated to the Marine Corps way of life. A change from U.S. Navy to U.S. Marine Corps uniform is required, and corpsman underwent a transformation that was considered "life changing" and Life saving.

The Draftees

Conscription in the United States, also known as **the draft**, has been used by the federal government in five conflicts: The American Revolution, Civil War, World War one, World War two, The Korean War and the Viet Nam War. From nineteen forty until nineteen seventy three, young men were drafted to fill vacancies in the armed forces that could not be filled through voluntary means. Eventually the draft would end when our country moved to an all voluntary service. When young men were notified by mail that they had been selected for the draft, they could just wait until they received orders to a military base such as the U.S. Army, or elect to go into the Navy, Air force or Marine Corp, therefore getting a better choice for service and duty stations. In the case of my friends from Cleveland, Ohio they all joined the Navy and opted out for Hospital Corps School, the same destination that I had after boot camp.

I remember four of the draftees Jack, Barney, Moose and Ralph. Another draftee named Scanlon a few years older than the guys from Cleveland was instrumental in motivating me towards gaining more education and knowledge. His father was a chiropractor and Scanlon had spent some time in college preparing for a medical career with his father. We played pool and watched T.V. in the barracks, and went on liberty together in several areas. They were all in their early twenties, and I was just turning eighteen. They showed me how to handle bullies that lived in the barracks and treated me like a kid brother. In the Navy at seventeen, the draftees that I worked with taught me basic hygiene, and how to fold my clothes in accordance with Navy regulations, and store them neatly in my locker.

Basic Life Lessons

As a young man, I did not have a mentor for basic personal growth. I attended grade school at Moulton Elementary, located in the small rural community of Moulton Ohio. Looking back at my high school peers in Wapakoneta, Ohio, many of them became factory or farm workers and traveled a different path through life. My favorite teacher in Middle school (Moulton), was a male teacher named Mr. Arthur. He was recently discharged from the army and had a teaching degree. He would often relate his military experience to the discipline required in school. He was a very quiet person and easy to talk to.

Very few of the young people that I knew from high school went on to college or had interest in a professional career. Before entering the Navy I had hung out at a bar/restaurant called *El Rancho* owned by Bud and Mag Goodwin, my god parents. local servicemen home on leave or recently discharged veterans frequented the restaurant simply known as *Buds Place.* I would often hear stories of where they had traveled to, good times and fun things they had experienced. Many of the veterans seemed to have regret for not staying in long enough to qualify for a retirement pension. At the age of twelve I helped in the restaurant washing dishes and busing tables. During construction of the restaurant I was asked to help pull electrical wires through the ceiling by climbing a ladder and crawling around the area above the ceiling. My nick name in those days was Stump because I was the smallest of the pre-teen kids. Bud and his brother Frank (Doc Goodwin), watched me carefully as I crawled through the overhead, pulling the wires to the opening in the ceiling for the lights.

Hospital Corps School

Once I had completed basic training in the Navy at the U.S. Naval Training Center at Great Lakes, Illinois (Boot Camp) I received my orders to a Service School, (Hospital Corps School), also located at Great Lakes Naval Training center. The program was considered as a basic "A" school for all hospital corpsman. Soon after starting Corps School, I met Rick Daffron. He and I went on liberty every other night and every other weekend.

This was known as Port and Starboard Liberty (every other night and every other weekend off). Port and starboard liberty was standard aboard ships at this time, and we were being indoctrinated to the Navy way of life. Rick and I came up with a plan on how to get around during our time off, we teamed up with two Air Force men that were also doing medical training at the time, and were off on the opposide nights and week ends. For example, Rick and I were assigned to the Port liberty section and the Airforce students were in he Starboard section. A few years later the Air force would establish their own training program. The four of us enjoyed our liberty and shared the car for trips to North Chicago, just outside of the base. We visited Milwaukee on week ends, toured breweries, and would double date or attend dances at "The Roof" on Saturday nights.

After six months of training I received orders to the U.S. Naval Hospital Great Lakes, Illinois. Upon arrival at the hospital I was directed to the personnel department at the Hospital where I was assigned to Ward 3-A, a neurosurgical care service. The patients were from all branches of the military and had serious conditions including spinal cord injuries, or brain pathology that impaired their everyday functions. My duties included handing out medications, assisting patients in and out of bed and assisting paralyzed patients. We had a few patient that had severe injuries causing paralysis from the neck down and several other patients suffering from various neurological disorders.

My first encounter with a paralyzed patient occurred in 1956 with a patient named Michael, an Army PFC home on leave waiting to be discharged from the Army (The Naval Hospital at Great Lakes, Illinois provided health care sevices for all branches of the military.)

It appeared that Michael was swimming in Lake Michigan when he dove into shallow water striking his head on the bottom causing fractures of his cervical vertebrae. Treatment in those days was conserative, and usually started with placing the patient on a stryker frame, that permitted the patient to be turned every few hours, from back to stomach. We did this as a team of corpsman, being careful not to tangle the drainage tubes and I.V lines that had been placed in the patient. One of the best corpsman I ever met was a guy named Scanlon, from Pennylvania. His father was a licensed Chiropractor and Scanlon (last name), was drafted in 1956 due to the fact that he was not currently enrolled in the school of Chiropractic. He was very mature, was married and was doing two years of active duty in the Navy. His medical education in Chiropractic gave him more skills than the average corpsman.

Scanlon was already working on the ward that I was assigned to. He was well liked by the staff and patients, and used his knowledge of patient care to assist in making patents comfortable. After a week or so, Scanlon started to giving me advice on completing my high school diploma. He directed me to the office where I could get the information to get started.

After working hours I studied in the barracks and usually did this in the company of the other draftees. Most were college educated and very helpful to me while studying. My Corpsman buddies and I worked as a team to rotate Michaels Stryker Frame to a different every 2-4 hours depending on the doctors orders at the time. Although it was uncomfortable, Michael never complained. We knew that he had hopes of recovery from his condition and did our best to keep his spirits up. Several of the medical wards treated serious and critical military patients that had been injured during their tour of active duty. Several of the patients being treated were veterans of the Korean War. I witnessed my first epileptic seizure on ward 3-A.

A group of service men were playing cards in the *solarium,* a room just off the main ward for patients to sit and relax. As I walked into the solarium, there was a loud noise as the card table was flipped over in the air and chairs and playing cards spread out over the room. One of the patients that had been playing cards had apparently suffered a Grand Mal Seizure and was flailing around on the floor. One of the other corpsman on duty had seen what happened and responded with wooden tongue depressors that were wrapped in gauze. He immediately forced the tongue depressors into the patients mouth, with the intention of preventing injury to the patients tongue. Years later, this procedure would be changed to simply moving furniture or other objects away from the patient to avoid injuries.

Medical Corpsman were trained to pass medications to patients and provide assistance using wheel chairs or carts when necessary. Critically injured or ill patients were provided with a private room and medical caere twenty four seven. During the night time hours, corpsman rotated on four hour shifts to ensure al o the patients nursing needs were provided. The first watch started at 4:00 pm or 16:00, going until 8:00 pm or 20:00 (twenty hundred) So we had 4-8 pm, 8-12 pm, 12:pm until 4:00 am or 0400 hours. The last watch was 0400-0800 hours and then the day crew took over. If you missed a few hours sleep during the night, you were not compensated and additional pay or time off, and just had to work until the end of your regular shift. The charge nurse on the unit you were assigned was authorized to let you leave the shift early if staffing would permit.

Living Quarters

All Corpsman shared the same barracks for living quarters. As an E-3 HN (hospitalman), I was at the lower end of the totem pole as they used to say. E-3 corpsman were quartered in small cubicles that provided a set of bunk beds and two lockers. HM2 or E-5 were quartered in private or semi private rooms. Barracks were basic wooden structures that had been built during World War 2. We had a community bathroom and shower that usually accomodated aproximately twenty five men. There was a lobby where we could buy snacks from a vending machine and soda available from a large cooler when you deposited coins.

A week after I arrived, I noticed that the soda cooler had empty bottles in it. Apparently, some of the new corpsman had figured out a way to get free soda. All corpsman working on hospital wards had access to plastic tubing for various medical applications. It did not take long for the new group of corpsman to figure out that the plastic tubing could be used for a straw at the soda machine. The barracks lobby also provided a pool table, a ping pong table, and an area for watching television. Washers and dryers were also provided in the bathroom and shower area. Corpsman were expected to maintain clean and neat uniforms, regardless of the season, or area where they were assigned. Summer white uniforms, t-shirts, skivvies (underwear), and socks could be laundered by each corpsman.

North Chicago

When things got boring in the barracks, young sailors headed to the nearest area where pizza, hoagies, and drinks could be found. The area just outside the main gates of the Great lakes Naval Base was known as North Chicago. In this area you could get food, drinks, entertainment, tatoos and meet friendly young ladies. Just to the east of this area, a short bus ride would take you to Waukegan, Illinois. Waukegan is thirty miles north of Chicago and is half way between Chicago and Milwaukee. North Chicago was convenient as a quick get away from the barracks, where one could get a pizza and a beer while listening to the music that was popular at the time. Chicago and Milwaukee were more popular on the week ends and the North shore line ran all day and night back in the day.

The North Shore line ran between Chicago and Milwukee and was a very inexpensive method of transportation. I spent a lot of my week ends off in Ohio and Indiana. I could get a round trip train ticket for $8.50, leaving from Chicagos Union Station going to Brazil, Indiana or Lima, Ohio. My girlfriend Angie Nichols was usually avalable on week ends, and we would take in a movie and have fun together. On Sunday night I would take a train back to Chicago's Union station and then walk a couple of blocks to the North Shore Line. There were always other sailors returning around the same time and we would walk to the North Shore line together.

Chicago's Union Station circa 1955

Chicago at night. 1950s

It is a natural tendency for people moving on foot through unfamiliar territory to band together. The buddy system is defined as: "a cooperative arrangement whereby individuals are paired or teamed up and assume responsibility for one another's instruction, productivity, welfare or safety". In my twenty years of travel with the Navy around the world, I could see this behavior in other branches of the military including the British Navy in North Hampton England, the Spanish Navy in various Mediterranean ports, and several other branches of the military around the world.

Using the Buddy System

Safety was always a concern in Chicago so we used the "buddy system" while traveling to the North Shore line station in Chicago's loop area. One late Sunday evening as I left Union Station I joined a small group of other sailors in uniform that apparently were headed for the North Shore Line. Our group consisted of three younger sailors such as myself and one older guy with three stripes. As we made our way up State street, we were met by the usual group of homeless guys, looking for a handout. As usual they spread out and blocked the sidewalk. The older guy in our group said "watch this" and then threw a hand full of coins out into the middle of State Street. Brakes squealed and horns honked as the homeless guys ran into the street.

I was frozen in my tracks fearing that someone would get hit. After a few seconds we quickly moved on up State street to catch our ride at the North Shore Line. Approaching the station, I always looked through the waiting area trying to find a familar face from the Naval Hospital. On there would usually be at least one sailor asleep on the bench and someone would wake him up in time to catch the train.

Friends we made on these week end trips, and young sailors like myself learned valuable lessons from the older "more salty" guys. Returning to base, we were anxious to find a place to eat and take a break from our trip. The enlisted dining area (chow hall) was usually closed by five pm, so we found the nearest "Roach Coach" to get a sandwich and drink. Roach coach was the name of the mobile canteen that was found around the base area. It was formally known as the mobile canteen, and was a large truck or van that moved around the base selling sandwiches, drinks and snacks.

Eating on base

Needless to say, the Navy chow hall otherwise known as the Enlisted Mens Mess Hall, was the cheapest place to eat. Although the U.S. Navy is well known for good food, you had to comply with some basic regulations:

1. You had to be dressed in the appropriate uniform of the day. You could not just walk in wearing your pajamas and expect to be served.
2. You must remove your hat upon entering the chow hall and getting in line. There was also a uniform way to fold your cover (hat) and place it in your belt.
3. No clowning around or grab ass while standing in line.
4. The chow hall was overseen by a senior petty officer wearing a badge. He was known as the Master at Arms. His job was to maintain order in the chow hall. If you misbehaved, you would be told to leave. Any objections were dealt with by the Master at arms or his deputies.
5. The chow hall was open during late hours 11 pm – 1:00 am for the night crew.

On Base Services

The U.S. Naval Base at great Lakes Illinois offered several on base activities, including bowling, movies, and a large gymnasium for working out. Most gyms were run by the special services department and provided organized physical activity including basketball, and baseball. The Naval Hospital in Philadelphia also organized deep sea fishing events off the coast of New Jersey. Hospital patients and staff enjoyed the trips. While stationed at the Naval Hospital in Philadelphia, I worked as a Chief Petty Officer organizing these trips as well as other on base activity for staff and patients. This activity took place during the Viet Nam conflict and several of our patients were amputees. Outings such as fishing trips were very important to improving the mental health of our patients.

Although Corpsman were trained for the medical aspects of their field, many of us were cross trained to handle more that first aid and minor surgery. Enlisted men clubs were the most popular form of group activity on base. The clubs usually provided good food and entertainment at a low cost.

Hospital Corps School USN

Bud at 17 years old

Hospital Corps School ("A School") was my first sevice school in the Navy. I was an E-3 (HN – Hospitalman) at the time. Later as an E-6 (HM1 Hospitalman First Class) I would complete B School or Advance Hospital Corps School, also known as Independent Duty School. The curriculum of this school qualified the Corpsman to serve aboard a ship without the benefit of a doctor on board and you were the *Medical Department Representative.*

In short I could do first aid and minor surgery, peform routine lab work and x-rays with my own equipment and while in port I could refer patients to a doctor at the hospital or dispensary. Suturing was a good skill to have, especially when sailors returned to the ship with lacerations from a bar room brawl, or a new cook had a bad cut.

I could diagnose and treat several ailments and kept the crew in good health. B school lasted for approximately six months, and was full time hours Monday through Friday. By the time I was ready to retire, I had also completed X-ray school, Nuclear, Biological, and Chemical Warfare School, plus instructors school. I was a multiskilled corpsman, and had numerous skills for any duty station assignment.

On Liberty in Chicago and Milwaukee

Watching the news in 2018 or 2019, you can see the historical differences that have occurred in regards to individual or group safety. For example, when my shimates Jack, Barney, Moose and Ralph and I went to Chicago, we visited several different parts of town, including the southern part of Chicago. We all liked jazz music, especially the clubs that featured black musicians. On at least one occassion we were in civilian clothes near a black club when a plain clothes police officer pulled up along the curb and asked where we were going. When we said we were headed for a club, he informed us that we were in the "wrong part of town" and then sped away. We continued on our way and had a great time. The folks running the club and their customers treated us well and we always enjoyed the visit.

Beer and Tattoos in Milwaukee

Sailors from the Great Lakes Naval Station loved Milwaukee for several reasons including the fact that Schlitz beer was manufactured there and was a strong competitor for Pabst (Pabst Blue Ribbon). The breweries offered free tours with samples of their products. Small groups of sailors were regular attendees at the breweries. It was always a good starting point for a week end of liberty. From the breweries we would gather at a favorite restaurant and then head for a local bar or head for our favorite dance hall known as "The Roof"

The History of Tattoos

In the summer of 1956 I received my first tattoo. Two of my friends from the Naval Base accompanied me to tattoo parlor in downtown Milwaukee. I had decided on a Navy anchor on my upper right arm along with my military service number placed directly over the anchor. As I grew older I began to realize that tattoos had historically been considered as a bad omen in the United States. The first electric tattoo machine was invented and patented in 1891 by Irish tattooist Samuel O'Reilly. Prior to this tattoos were applied using needles or other sharp instruments that were dipped in various colors of ink. The earliest tattoos that we know of ae from 5000 years ago and were found on the body of "iceman" from the Italian – Austrian borders. Greeks learned tattooing from the Persians annd used it to mark slaves and criminals so they could be identified if they tried to escape. Romans in turn adopted the practice from the Greeks, and in late antiquity when the Roman army consisted largely of mercenaries; they were also tattooed so that deserters could be identified. In the twentieth century, tattos became more controversial. While teaching college at Sinclair Community College in Dayton, Ohio; I taught Radiology classes and did clinical supervision at three different hospital. One of the hospitals, Good Samaritan, was one of the first to have issues with tatoos and body piercing. Tatoos for employees was not acceptable if the tatoo showed on the neck. Body piercing required a written waiver from the patient if the piercing was in the same area as the body part being x-rayed. The radiologist were concerned that the metallic piercing device could conceal an area of interest. The staff at Miami Valley Hospital informed my students that they had adopted policy regarding tatoos. Students would not be considered for employment if their tatoo showed on the neck. The concern was that several gang members were displaying tatoos on their neck to identify a specific gang.

Navy Tattoos

Since the Navy introduced tatoos into the general U.S. culture in the early 1900's, they have become a long time tradition in this branch of the armed forces. Compared to others branches, they have the highest propensity towards tattooing.

In the Loop

Down in the loop as It was known, you could always count on seeing a lot of sailors in uniform on the week ends. Most of them were from sevice schools that were located north of Chicago at the U.S. Naval Training Center, Great lakes. On my last visit to Michigan Avenue, Jack, Moose and I were taking in the sights when we observed a large group of sailors running from the drug store across the street. Apparently several of them were in on a scam for free food. Here is how it worked: At least six sailors in uniform would gradually take a seat at the lunch counter in Walgreens.

After ordering and finishing their meal, they would rapidly depart the lunch counter on a predetermined signal. Once on the sidewalk, they would blend in with the sea of uniformed sailors. A confused store manager ran out of the store and simply shrugged his shoulders with his arms out. The guys that I hung out with were to mature and honest to do anything like this.

While in Chicago one week end, Jack, and Moose convinced us to visit the Playboy Club. I was only 18 and I was permitted to drink draft beer, however my "big brothers" would not let the bunnies sit on my lap. I was disappointed and took a lot of kidding from my buddies. Shortly after this I received orders for the U.S. Naval Hospital in Yokosuka, Japan. Two other corpsman from the Naval Hospital at Great Lakes received orders at the same time, John Campbell HN and Gabby Miller HN. I would meet them in a few weeks after my departure, and we would work together and enjoy the good times in Japan.

Heading West for Japan

After completing my first two years of active duty at the Great Lakes Naval Hospital, I was shipped out to the U.S. Naval Hospital in Yokosuka, Japan. I was given options of driving, flying or taking a train. Train was my choice. I wanted to see as much of the United States as possible and thought that a long train ride would be interesting. I headed for San Francisco in the summer of 1957. Boarding a train in Lima, Ohio (only 12 milkes from my hometown of Wapakoneta, Ohio), I transferred to a train in Chicago that would take me all the way to the west coast. It was an interesting trip and everyone was friendly and talkative. I wish they would have had cell phones back in the day. The scenary was great and little did I realize that this would be my last cross country train ride. In years to come I would revisit the west coast and Las Vegas via airlines.

The train was a comfortable ride, the food was decent and there were a few other sailors in uniform also headed for San Francisco. I was an E3 with two years service and the other guys were older and had a few more stripes. We played cards, read magazines and got to know each other. As soon as we arrived in San Francisco, we shared a cab to the receiving barracks, located at Treasure Island, California.

Treasure Island has quite a history. It has been used by the Navy since World War II. On my arrival in 1957, it provided temporary housing for me and hundreds of other sailors that were in transit from one duty station to the next. Built in 1936-1937, T.I. as we called it had several functions over the years. It is currently listed on the National Registry of Historical Places, and closed on September 30th 1997.

Visiting Tijuana Mexico

Tijuana Mexico 1957

My stay on Treasure island only lasted for about two weeks, and included a couple of interesting trips to Tijuana Mexico. Sailors that had been staying there for a while invited me on a bus trip, so a group of about eight of us headed across the border. No passports were needed just a valid Military I.D. card. There were bars restaurants everywhere and close to where our bus let us off.

My instincts told me to stay clear of the bars. You could hear the music and laughter as soon as you stepped of the bus. A few of us headed towards what they referred to as the tourist area, where you could buy souvenirs. After having dinner in a local restaurant, three of us headed back to the bus stop. The return trip was not as nice as the trip down. Unfortunately some of the sailors did not hold their drinks to well and got sick on the way back. Our driver was prepared for this and had a supply of "Barf Bags"on hand. Little did I realize at the time; that as a Navy Corpsman I would be dealing with drunken sailors on a regular basis, epecially aboard the ships that I would serve on.

Fortunately, there were no border issues in 1957, and no drug problems that we see today. The ride back gave the sailors time to sober up. Border patrol did come aboard the bus to check our I.D. cards and we went on our way back to Treasure Island. When I look back on the places I visited in Chicago, Milwaukee, San Francisco, and Tijuana, I know that the security and safety that I enjoyed will never be the same. As my travels continued over the next eighteen years, I will learn to appreciate the world that we live in and always be prepared for the inevitable change.

Leaving California

From Teasure Island, I was bused along with five other sailors to Travis Air Force Base, fifty three miles north of San rancisco. It was a short ride and we were quickly loaded on to a Large military aircraft that was apparently used routinely for transporting military personnel. We sat in what appeared to be a cargo net, not exactly riding in coach or first class, we knew that our ride would get us to our destination. Unlike commercial airline flights, we did not check in our luggage. Sailors in my day were issued "sea bags" that were capable of carrying all standard issue clothing that you were required to have. We had been trained in boot camp to pack a sea bag by folding each item according to the specifications that we had been taught. My sea bags would eventually be replaced by a nice set of luggage as I gained stripes.

Our first stop after leaving Travis Air Force base was Hickam Air force Base in Hawaii. The plane was refueled and we all had a chance to get breakfast in the Air Force cafeteria. We had a short time to stretch our legs and look around before heading back to the plane. The weather was very warm and humid and we could feel the warm tropical breezes as we walked around the terminal area. We eventually departed for Tokyo, Japan stopping briefly at a Wake island to refuel before completing our flight to Tokyo.

Arriving in Tokyo/Yokosuka

It was an exhausting trip and we were glad to set foot on solid ground. We were placed aboard a military bus and headed out to various military bases between Tokyo and Yokosuka. We arrived at our final destination late in the afternoon and were then escorted to our barracks and personal cubicle. Each cubicle consisted of a large set of bunk bed, two lockers and a desk. The beds were comfortable and I fell asleep quickly. The barracks were occupied by hospital corpsman and anyone holding the rank of E-5 or above was provided with a semi private or private room. Japanese houseboys provided housecleaning duties including linen changes. Shortly after arrival, I met up with John Wayne Campbell and Gabby Miller, two of my best friends from the Naval Hospital at Great lakes. Eventually I would have several close friends from the area of the barracks that I resided in.

Yokosuka Harbour

The 7th Fleet in Yokosuka Japan

The Navy's 7th fleet was headquarted in Yokosuka, Japan. Yokosuka provided support to the fleet which consisted of 60-70 ships, 300 aircraft, and 40,000 Navy and Marine personnel. Most of the ships were usually underway and maintained operations on a daily basis, however on some occassions, the fleet was in, meaning the downtown area of Yokosuka was flooded with sailors an Marines. The bars and stores loved the influx of sailors however the local military residents stayed away until the crowds diminished. Occasionally an aircraft carrier would arrive with a crew of about 6,000 and needless to say Yokosuka became very crowded. The enlisted mens club was located in downtown Yokosuka. A Military I.D. Card was required for admission, and you were permitted to bring a guest. Several sailors would bring a date from one of the local bars. Behind the club, where prostitutes thrived, penicillin tablets were handed out as a prophylactic. Years later this practice was discontinued when it was proven that penicillin became less effective when used with high frequency.

Hanging out with the guys

The Naval base had numerous activities such as bowling, movies, shopping, fishing and sail boats. The dowTntown activity in the enlisted men club was very attractive with the close proximity, and only 70 yen of Japanese currency at the time (about .50 cents). The club had live entertainment nightly, a Navy Exchange selling all types of merchandise, including liquor, cigarettes (about $2.00 a carton in the 50's), plus great restaurants. The military police were kept busy by the female guest trying to get their boyfriends to buy cigarettes and booze for them. A short walk from the Enlisted mens club was the infamous Skivvy alley, famous for bars, shops, black market sales, prostitutes and crowded streets. It was not unusual to see a corpsman or chaplin handing out penicillin tablets to help combat venereal diseases. A corpsman I knew named Parrot was often handing out religious material encouraging young men to attend the Christian Center not to far from the downtown area. Tatoos parlors were among the more well attended activities. It was here that I received my second tattoo on my left upper arm to balance out the anchor on my right upper arm. A few months later I received my final tattoo, a sailing ship on my chest. This was the most painful since there was not much tissue on the thorax (chest area). I healed slowly and had no signs of infection. The tattoo artist were very clean and meticulous when applying tattoos. In my two years of residence in Japan, I found that the japanese polulation in general were very courteous, kind and polite. Traveling by train with the general population, I was often amazed by their generosity and traditions that had been handed down for centuries. When visiting someones home, you took off your shoes and left them at the door.

Before eating, you were usually handed a warm moist towel to clean your hands with. In a few weeks my navy buddies that had arrived in Japan about the same time that I did were all speaking Japanese and practicing on each other. Bar girls, waiters, store clerks and others were all impressed with our rapid transformation. The houseboys in our barracks also contributed to our increase in knowledge. The hospitals medical staff of MD's and nurses (RN's) were all americal citizens, however the interns and residents were all Japanese. Very nice people who were willing to answer qustions from a young Navy Corpsman. I also learned about acupuncture, a form of medical practice being used in Asian contries that would not be in practice for several more years in the United States. I retained some of this knowledge that I have used over the years.

Not all fun and games

There were bad times as well as good. Although I worked on a medical ward, there were times when the hospital Emergency Room became ovewhelmed. During my second year at the hospital, I was temporarily sent to the X-ray department to assist with taking x-rays of a helicopter crew that had crashed nearby. It was my first time dealing with any serious trauma. I assisted moving patients on and off the table and positioning each patient when necessary. I found this intriguing, and eventually signed on for x-ray school when I reenlisted. My good buddy "mouse" succumbed to a fatal illness after he was admitted to one of the contagion wards. Initially diagnosed with encephalitis, mouse was a small and fragile person who was liked by everyone on the hospital compound. During my last year of service in Yokosuka, the corpsman were asked to help stand guard at the hospitals mortuary. We were informed that someone had been breaking in to the hospital morgue, raping and molesing corpse that were kept there. Necrophilia is described as an erotic attraction to corpses. The guard duty was eventually discontinued when the culprit was found and prosecuted. The corpsman that I knew from the hospital seemed to work well together and liked to hang out in small groups while on liberty. Base Special services offered week end getaways in the mountainous regions of Japan. The hotel provided spacious and luxurious rooms at a very low price. Restaurants at the hotel were excellent and provided fantastic meals. Our favorite hotel was a located fairly close to Mt. Fuji and was one of the finest hotels that I had ever visited.

Nearby the hotel there were trout streams and guest were able to check out fishing gear for the day. John Campbell and I each caught a few decent sized trout. We were pemitted to bring our catch back to the hotel where they were pepared for us and served for dinner at a pre-arranged time. After dinner the hotel had live entertainment which completed a perfect day.

Trout fishing in the mountains of Japan

Rice is a Japanese staple

As we headed back to Yokosuka from our week end of R and R, (rest and relaxation) we reflected on the fun that we had. We were riding a train that would take us directly to Yokosuka and were enjoying the countryside view. A couple of the guys were eating cooked rice from a metal container, which was a common staple among the Japanese people. Rice could be purchased in many forms in japan, however the canned rice was very popular at railway stations. The guys eating rice were John and Ferris. The folks watching them eat were very impressed by their ability to eat with chop sticks, and their smiling faces told the whole story. We had all been in country for at least a year, and we all knew the traditions and customs that persisted among the Japanese people.

Tokyo's Ginza has been the city's top shopping district for several years. Ginza is packed with upscale boutiques and sushi bars. American sevicemen from military bases throughout Japan frequent the Ginza to shop and explore the area. High end electronics are currently a hot product in this area. Night life in Tokyo is very well known as well as the upscale restaurants and world famous theatres. I recall buying souveneirs to take back home to Ohio such as a pool cue for playing billiards. Older brother Pete loved to play pool back in Wapakoneta, Ohio and he loved the handcrafted pool cue that I brought back home in 1959. I also brought back two hand crafted jewelry boxes. I kept one for a souvenir and gave one to my mother.

Tokyo's Ginza circa

Leaving Japan

In the summer of 1959, I received orders to return to the United States.

Fortunately, my ride home was already in Yokosuka, Japan, The USS Dixie was ready to pull up their anchor and head back to their home port of SanDiego California. I had been staying at the receiving barracks on base, peforming mundane task while waiting for my orders back home. Instead of flying back to the states, I was in fact taking a real Navy cruise. It was a very exciting time for me and the three other sailors that joined me when boarding the ship. When we reported aboard for temporary duty, we were shown the proper way to board a ship. First you saluted the Ameican flag that was on the ships fantail (back of ship), then looked at the O.O.D. (officer of the deck), asked permission to come aboard while saluting him. The USS Dixie was a well known ship, she served the country for 42 years, until decomissioned on June 15, 1982. After reporting aboard, I was escorted to sick bay where the petty oficer in charge showed me to the bething area. Our quarters in sick bay were very comfortable; not the usual canvas rack with a thin pad to use as a mattress.

My first meal was breakfast, and it was better than I had hoped for. The Dixie had a very large chow hall and everything was easily accessible. The four of us that were working our way back to the states sat with the regular crew of corpsman. Ater brief introductions, we had a great meal and the meals in the following weeks was just as good. Once undeway, we were all assigned specific duties such a helping inventory supplies, prepare lab test, assist developing xrays, and house keeping duties. We would reach Hawaii in just a few day, and were ready for liberty.

Hawaii, Circa 1959

Enjoying the Island

It was late July 1959, and my four year enlistment was ending soon. The four of us decided to rent a car, do the beach first and then head out to explore the island. None of us had ever tried to use a surf board, however we decided to do it. After watching people surf while we were having a beer at a table with an umbrella, we finally decided to give it a try. Although we only had a few beers each,we were ready. We paddled out a little way then gradually got up on the board and just hung on as long as we could. I don't remember who fell first, it did not matter, we were having a great time. After a couple of hours we did lunch and headed out in the car. We were all impressed by the islands beauty. Rob was the most excited about the possibility of staying in Hawaii and possibly starting up a small business on the beach. Upon our arrival at the ship he went to the personnel department and made a formal request to transfer to the Naval Base to complete his remaining time in Hawaii. His request was granted and he was off the ship when we got underway for San Diego. My time in San Diego was brief and I was back in Ohio within the week. I started dating my future wife Beverly shortly after taking up residence in Wapakoneta, Ohio, only ten miles from St.Marys (Beverly's home). I worked at the Omar Bread Company for two months and then decided to reenlist in the Navy. Once discharged, I had three months to reenlist without losing a reenlistment bonus of approximtely three thousand dollars, plus my choice of schools. I chose X-ray school, something my dad had recommended years earlier.

U.S. Naval Hospital Philadelphia

After choosing X-Ray school, I was informed that I would be going to Philadelphia for my x-ray training. Bev and I were excited about starting a new life in a big city. Once we were settled in to our new apartment, we located the hospital, only a few block away from our new location. The Philadelphia Naval Hospital Was the first high-rise hospital building constructed by the U.S. Navy. In 1935 it opened as a state of the art facility with 650 beds and a total floor space 352,000 square feet. The central building was 15 floors high and my radiology department was on the third floor. The hospital was situated on 49 acres and included ground level structures that ran for blocks adjacent to the hospital. During the Viet Nam conflict, the wards were used to house amputees and mental health patients. The enormity of this complex required the security staff to patrol on electric scooters.I reported in on a Monday and met the other five corpsman that would be my classmates. The names I remember are Brooks, Honald, Melton, Lucas and Abershon. The program did not officially start until January 1st, 1960, so we were officially classified as working O.J.T. or on the job training. The program was twelve months long, and we graduated on January 2nd, 1961. Unfortunately Lucas did not make it through the program. About six months into the program, Lucas was having problems staying awake during the day. Seems he had taken a part time job to improve his income, however on one particular day while the working with the head Radiologist his slow performance was noticed. Lucas was told by the radiologist to meet him in his office. About 10-15 minutes later when the radiologist (also a navy captain) came to his office, he found Lucas asleep in his chair near the desk, and we could hear the captain yelling in the main hallway even though his office was down the hall and around the corner. That was the last day for Lucas. In the past he had been caught sleeping in the dark room when the techs were not getting any response when they placed film cassettes in the dark room pass box for developing.

The Radiology Program (X-ray school)

My class consisted of five students after Lucas was forced to drop out. We all felt bad for him, however we realized how the Navy or any other military organization feels about sleeping on duty. He eventually returned to the fleet and we never heard from him again. The program was excellent, and Radiographers were in great demand. We soon learned that we were in a predominantly female occupation, that favored male techs as supervisors. This would change in later years. Our our original class consisted 6 sailors. We would lose one class mate (Lucas) as I mentioned earlier. Our workday began with morning muster (Calling attendance). There were approximately twenty staff X-ray techs working in the department plus 5 students. There were seven rooms of diagnostic x-ray equipment, portable xrays, surgical xrays, plus techs also covered the file room and check in desk. Every morning we were required to line up in the hallway while the chief called our names. After attendance was completed we were informed of any special notices for that day, or upcoming inspections.

HM2 Bobby Brown was the clown of the crew. One Friday around noon, he asked the chief if it would be ok if he went to the commissary to pick up a few items. The chief replied "no problem". It was summertime and the chief suggested that Bobby should park in the shade when he is done shopping, Bobby replied "no problem. We did not see Bobby again until Monday. He had parked in the shade after shopping; Bobby lived in Maple Shade New Jersey and had simply went home.

Working as a Staff Radiographer

Bobby was aware of the fact that we usually were dismissed early on Fridays, so just headed for home. Actually, the chief had a great sense of humor, so Bobby lucked out. The regular shift ended at 4:00 pm or 16:00 hours. The chief or a designated supervisor would walk through the department and announce "we are setting the watch", meaning that the duty crew is now taking over and everyone else is free to leave. The hospital accepted any type of military patient or their dependents. Retired military were welcome and on occasion, we would take chest x-rays of cadets from the military schools such as Annapolis. The Naval Base was located directly south of the hospital on Broad Street, so the majority of our active duty military patients came from the base. One of the most interesting experiments that occurred involving our x-ray techs working on the Naval Base would have to include the use of x-rays during experiments that were used to determine the impact of pilot ejections from their planes. Apparently the force of injection could adversely affect the spine, so a series of events were recorded using x-ray videos of the spine during ejection. The end results assisted in designing improved ejection methods that would lessen injuries that could occur. In July 1960, I was working in The Radiology when we were told that a blimp from Lakehurst, New Jersey had crashed with twenty one men on board. When the news first broke, it was reported that there was at least one dead and three injured and 21 missing. Long story short, there were three dead bodies brought to the Naval Hospital in Philadelphia. Apparently there were more found dead among the missing. Our job as x-ray techs. was to x-ray the bodies to look for any signs of foul play such as bullets or shrapnel. It was a very long day, bringing back memories of the Navy flyers that I helped xray after the helicopter crash in Japan.

Lake Hurst, N.J. Blimp

Personnel Inspections

Although we were stationed in a large metropolitan area, we were frequently reminded that we were an integral part of a military organization. In order to ensure that the staff was prepared for deployment, inspections were held on a regular basis. *Junk on the bunk* was held in the barracks. You were required to display all of your government issued clothing such as underwear, socks, shoes, t-shirts, summer white uniforms, and navy blue winter uniforms. All items had to be folded as shown in the Blue Jackets manual. Failure to pass inspection required an additional inspection at a designated time. The chief would walk through the barracks passing by the end of each bed, making notes. *Personnel inspections* usually occured on Fridays in the early afternoon. Normally, there would be a group of forty to fifty people being inspected, all wearing the prescribed uniform, complete with ribbons or medals. This was always an impressive event.

Living in Philadelphia

We lived just a few blocks away from the hospital and had easy access to the Naval Base and commissary, however we were advised by an Italian friend (Tom Lucas) that it would be more economical to shop at an area known as the Italian Market, also known as the open air market. Most of the people that I knew were lower ranking military men and we tried to shop wisely on a small paycheck. The Italian Market ran approximately ten city blocks along ninth street in South just a few blocks from were we lived. Dozens of vendors line the street selling fresh vegetables, meat and fish. Gourmet shops and restaurants occupied the storefronts in between. Bev and I had our first cheesesteak sandwich here, never hearing of this back in Ohio.

Philadelphia's Italian Market along 9th Street, approximately 10 blocks   The original Philly Cheesesteak

Family and Friends in Philadelphia

Each time we were stationed In Philadelphia, we made new friends. Our relatives in North philly remained in the same location and we would occasionally visit them, especially when my dad came to town. My dad would choose a restaurant and invite his sisters Eleanor and Mildred. They would always bring their husbands George and Freddy. We also made trips to Atlantic City with them and ejoyed the area. In Philly our first friends were all stationed at the hospital and worked in Radiology. Most of the X-ray people lived in Philly fairly close to the hospital, so it was convenient for get togethers. Patrick McArdle was a senior technologist when I was a radiology student. He lived in the same housing area, just a few blocks from our house. Approximately six of us resided within a few blocks of each other and often car pooled to and from the hospital. Car pooling made it convenient to stop at a local bar on the way home to play shuffle board and darts while enjoying a beer. Pat would call his wife Patricia and let her know that we were on our way home and she would inform my wife Bev. We always stopped at the same neighborhood bar where we were treated well. The fact that we were all Navy seemed to be a positive factor in our relationship. Whenever one of the guys received orders for transfer, the was a small party at the bar. We all felt like family during these events making a lot of nice memories.

Cuban Missile Crisis

At the end of my tour of duty in Philly, the *Cuban Missle Crisis* occurred. In October 1962, an American U2 spy plane secretly photographed **nuclear** missile sites being built by the Soviet Union on the island of Cuba. President Kennedy did not want the Soviet Union and Cuba to know that he had discovered the missiles. He met secretly with his advisors for several days to discuss the problem. Soviet premier Nikita Khrushchev had reached a secret agreement with Cuba's Fidel Castro to place Soviet nuclear missiles in cuba to deter any future invasion attempts such as the failed Bay of Pigs invasion. There was a major confrontation that brought the United States and the Soviet Union close to war over the presence of Soviet nuclear armed missiles in Cuba. At the time, I was assigned to a surgical team to be deployed in case there was an incident and casualties occurred. I met with the team and inventoried all of the medical and surgical supplies to be shipped out in the event of a war with Russia. It was a very scary time and thankfully a peaceful resolution was reached after the Navy intercepted the Russian ships headed for Cuba.

Aboard ship, inspections take on a more serious note. In addition to personnel inspections you must prepare for Operational Readiness Inspections and be prepared for the unexpected when heading out to sea on an extended cruise such as a mediterranean cruise or a carribean cruise. For example on my first ship assignment, the USS Rankin (AKA-103), our first O.R.I. (Operational Readiness Inspection), was conducted at the Guantanamo Naval Base in Cuba. The Rankin was a *Tolland-Class attack cargo ship.* Our motto was "Ready Now". She functioned as an amphibious warefare vessel, transporting men and equipment to combat areas to prepare for invasions or evacuations.

While in Cuba, the ship was anchored out in the bay and we would have an inspection team onboard daily to running us through drills and holding inventory. After going through our daily inspections and drills, we would all head to the Enlisted mens club located on the Naval base at Gitmo (Guantanamo Naval Base) We were anchored out in the bay, so we were taxied to the pier by small boats called Landing Crafts (LCM's). From the pier we were transported to the enlisted mens club with what was called "cattle cars". Cattle cars were trailers with standing room only. It was not unusual for some of the crew members to fall during the ride. I recall tending to bruises and bumps during sick call the next morning. We passed the O.R.I. inspection and deployed into the carribean sea.

USS Rankin (AKA-103)

The Rankin was a Tolland class attack cargo ship, made for amphibous landings, carying cargo and troops into hostile environments. On occasions, we would also carry a Seal Team to perform strategic missions whenever necessary. While I was on the Rankin, The seal team had a second class (HM2) corpsman with them. He and a couple of other seals would hang out in sick bay. I helped provide supplies for any upcoming missions and got to know a few of them. Our sick bay had a treatment room, small office with lab supplies and medications, plus an eight bed ward for patient recovery. It was not used very often, so the open area was used for socializing, coffee breaks and after hours card games.

Our medical staff consisted of eight Hospital Corpsman ranging from E-3 to E-7 in paygrade, plus one medical officer (doctor). "Sick call" was held every morning at 0800 hours and again at 13:00 hours (1:00 pm). Emergencies or injuries were seen at any time. A daily report was sent to the X.O. (excutive officer) on a daily basis informing him of anyone that had been placed on the binnacle list (sick list). Our Chiefs name was student. A very strict, no nonsense individual.

The other corpsman were Labonte, Gibbs, Strayer, Forbes, Burgess, and Hunton. We worked well as a team and often went on liberty together. One of the more memorable ports that we visited was San Juan Puerto Rico. We visited Morrow Castle shortly after our arrival. From the castle, we headed downtown to the tourist area. Hotels here were very expensive however this is where we found the best restaurants. Most of Puerto Rico appeared to be on the low end of the property scale. We found that the sailors and marines from most of the ships went to "Old Puerto Rico", where the cheap bars and prostitutes were found. These areas were patrolled by the Navy Shore Patrol, looking for anyone in uniform that may be misbehaving.

On liberty in Puerto Rico

The Rankin crew and the Seal Team all enjoyed the nice climate in Pueto Rico. One of the upscale hotels had a nice restaurant and bar just behind the hotel overlooking the harbor. Roger, Gibbs and I were at a table looking at the Rankin, anchored out in the water. We had been enjoying a beer when we heard a metallic sound against the wall where we were sitting. The stone wall was just a few feet high and a comfortable place to rest your feet. Three Navy Seals suddenly came over the wall in wet suits. We knew them immediately and pulled up a few chairs for them. We sat together and told sea stories for a couple of hours and then headed back to the ship. We went to the fleet landing and took the liberty boat back to the ship, the seals simply swam back. In the morning we got underway for our next assignment.

San Juan Puerto Rico, circa 1964

Morrow Castle – San Juan Puerto Rico

Squadron ExercisesOnSquadr

During squadron exercises in April 1965, *Rankin* participated in the Dominican Republic Intervention. Arriving off the coast of Santo Domingo, *Rankin* and other ships of PhibRon 10 commenced the mass embarkation and evacuation of over 1,000 refugees and U.S. civilian nationals. As a result of this operation, the *Rankin* and all her personnel were awarded the Navy Unit Commendation by the Secretary of the Navy. LCM's are made for combat, so their bullets bounced off the hull of our LCM as we proceeded to evacuate civilians. Aboard ship at sea it was a quiet lifestyle. We used our sickbay for card playing and good comradarie. The ships stewards would usually prepare sandwhiches for the sick bay (fortunately we never had anyone ill enough to require a bed.) We would tip the steward from the pot of cash on the card table. HM2 Gibbs, was our only black corpsman, and he was good friends with the stewards. Gibbs was always a bit overweight, so we all suspected that he had another source of food supply. All of the corpsman had friends in other divisions, and we would swap information and other favors as part of the sea going Navy tradition.

Leaving the Rankin- Headed for Camp Lejeune

In 1965, I reenlisted while aboard the Rankin and was reassigned to the first battalion, Eighth Marine Regiment, located with the second division at Camp Lejeune, North Carolina. This would be my first and last tour of duty with the marines, and since I had already completed eighteen months of sea duty aboard the USS Rankin (AKA-103), I would only have to serve eighteen months of Fleet Marine Duty. The rest of my company of corpsman would end of being shipped out about a year after I reported aboard. I would see several of my friends minus arms and legs when I returned to Philadelphia for my next tour of duty after leaving Camp Jejune, North Carolina.

History of Hospital Corpsman with the Marines

The U.S. Marine Corps was founded on November 7th, 1775 to conduct ship to ship fighting, provide shipboard security, discipline enforcement and assisted in landing forces in foreign countries. Hospital Corpsman have been assigned to the Marines since World War 2. Corpsman earned a total of 684 personal awards including 22 medals of honor, 55 Navy Crosses, and 236 Silver Stars. As of my retirement in 1975, Corpsman were the most highly decorated group in the Navy. Corpsman receive their training at Camp Lejeune, North Carolina. The training in my day was conducted at Camp Geiger, located in close proximity to Camp Jejune. Class room instruction and field exercises were held at Camp Geiger under the supervision of active duty marines that had recent combat experience in Viet Nam. Corpsman were issued Marine corps uniforms and equipment for the prior to the training process. The only distinguishing difference was the Navy rating badges that we wore on our marine uniform

Feet Marine Force Camp Lejune, North Carolina

Class room education was an introduction to the Marine Corps way of life, and how to survive in a combat situation. We did field orientation in wooded areas, including night time maneuvers, again with the emphasis on survival. We boarded a ship at Moorehead City and participated in Wet Net Training. Wet approached the Naval vessel from an LCM, went aboard wearing a full back pack and then proceeded to disembark from the side of the ship to an LCM waiting below. The so called "wet net" was just a series of ropes connected together to make a ladder down the side of the ship. A marine sergeant stood at the top of the net loudly giving instructions on how to safely go down the ladder. Non swimmers were identified by the white tape across the top of their helmet.

If a non swimmer fell from the ladder, he would be identified by the helmet floating at the base of the ladder with white tape on the top, and presumably the person falling from the ladder would be below the helmet. Once our training was completed, we were assigned to a Medical Company. I was an HM2 –E5. I had just one more stripe than most of my company.

USS Rankin

The USS Sandoval (APA-194)

Shortly after arrival at our first FMF assignment at Camp Jejeune, we were informed that we were scheduled for a Med Cruise. My fellow corpsman: Davis, Sherman, Shively, Obrien, and others felt a bit crowded in the berthing area. I had eight years service at the time and was due to take a test for E6 (HM1). I remember boarding the Sandoval in Moorehead City North Carolina. It was a very large ship and the crews quarters were dimly lit and the bunks were stacked five high. Fortunately for me, I passed my rating exam and was promoted to E6, equivalent to a Marine Staff NCO. I was transferred to the Staff NCO quarters located on the first deck of the ship. The bunks were only two high and we had much more living space. Plus much more lighting. In addition, we had our own area for dining. Although making E6 was an improvement, I missed the camaraderie of being with my group of corpsman. During regular work hours I spent time with our company of corpsman helping out in sick bay. Sandovals sick bay was one of the largest I had seen, with treatments rooms and several beds. The corpsman in our group appreciated the time we were able to spend in sick bay, getting to work topside instead of being on the lower decks.

Before heading back to the states, we visited Naples, Italy. The Sandoval was anchored in the harbor, so they ran smaller boats from the ship to the fleet landing in Naples. Chief Bullard and five of us went into town together, and the chief reminded us that Naples is also known as the city of thieves. We stayed in close proximity, using the buddy system while moving through the narrow streets, however we were being hustled and pulled by the wrist to see the sights. One of our corpsman suddenly realized that his wrist watch was missing. We then banded together more closely, and more aggressively pushed the hustlers away. A few guys picked up souvenirs to take home, and we ended up going back to the ship a little early to avoid a rush at the fleet landing. Most sailors that have traveled realize it is a good idea to head back to the ship early in order to avoid the drunks that gather at the fleet landing. Within a day or so after getting underway were headed back to Moorehead City, North Carolina.

The scuttlebutt was that our battalion was to deploy to Viet Nam. Within a day or so after returning to Camp Lejeune, we received official notification that we were in fact deploying to Viet Nam. While our company of corpsman were busy packing our gear to ship out, Chief Bullard approached me with good news: Since I already had over 18 months of sea duty aboard the USS Rankin, and my time with the Marines at Camp Lejeune also counted as sea duty, I had fulfilled my required 36 months of sea duty. I was now required to transfer to a shore duty assignment. I reported to headquarters and picked up my orders to the Naval Hospital, Philadelphia. This would be my second tour of duty at Philly. I took leave and headed back to Ohio with Bev and the girls for a visit with our relatives before heading to Philly.

Returning to the U.S. Naval Hospital Philadelphia

Bev stayed in Ohio while I went to Philly to arrange for housing. The hospital looked the same however government housing had been built just across the street from the hospital, and there was now an 18 hole golf course just to the south of our house. Our new home was an all brick structure with air, heat and plenty of space for our family. The Hospital's main gate was just one block away from our house. To our south side was a large city park with a small lake and ample areas for biking and hiking. Adjacent to the park was a fairly new 18 hole golf course that I would enjoy with guys from the Radiology Department. Chief McQuarter was my golf mentor and we played after working hours and week ends. One of the perks to living close to the golf course was finding golf balls along the side of the road near our house. By the time I left Philly I had collected a bucket full of balls. Veterans Stadium was located East of the hospital just off Broad Street, a main street running north and south through Philadelphia. The park near our house and Vets Stadium would play an important role in Beverly obtaining her Pennsylvania drivers license. She could practice driving in the park, with little or no traffic on the week ends, and then go down the street to Vets stadium to practice parking. She passed her driving test the first time around.

Philly 1966 - 1968

Now that I was working as a staff Radiologic Technologist with a couple of more stripes, my duties and responsibilities had changed. My boss was Chief McQuarter, the department chief and my golfing buddy. I was placed in charge of quality control, ensuring that all x-ray images were of good quality and that our repeat rate was as low as possible. It felt great to be in Philadelphia again, however some things never change, such as the Schuylkill Expressway; a two to eight lane freeway through Montgomery County and the city of Philadelphia, and the easternmost segment of interstate 76 in the state of Pennsylvania. At the hospital, we referred to it as the "the world's longest parking lot." HM2 John Stahler, HM1 Bob Cujas, HM2 Garrison, and a few other X-ray techs had also returned for another tour of shore duty. Most of us eventually took part time jobs taking x-rays at local hospitals. Unfortunately, some of my former shipmates from Camp Lejeune also showed up as patients in our X-ray department.

Walking through the department one afternoon, I heard someone calling my name from the area where patients on carts were placed while waiting to be x-rayed. Walking into the area, I found two hospital corpsman that I recognized from Camp Lejeune, North Carolina. Apparently, their medical company had been attacked shortly after their arrival in Viet Nam. They had just set up their field medical tent, when they were "fragged" by the enemy inflicting numerous casualties among the corpsman. Both of these young men had lost and arm and a leg during the attack, plus the younger man had lost his testicles when his leg was blown off. I felt very sad for them, however the youngest of the two was very cheerful, apparently he had managed to impregnate his wife shortly before leaving the states. At this point in time the Naval Hospital had become the amputee center for the east coast, and the ramps were full of amputees.

As an HM1, E-6, I no longer stood watch in the Radiology Department. As a senior petty officer, I was now required to rotate my duty nights as officer of the day, an administrative position, ensuring security for the hospital. The Viet Nam War was controversial and there had been bomb threats called into the hospitals front desk. I stood duty once a week and was required to stay at the hospital overnight as part of the duty requirement. I had to make rounds throughout the hospitals property which included the Amputee ramps and enlisted clubs. There were 6-8 other corpsman on duty to assist with situations such as fighting in the club, or amputees fighting with the staff. In order to cover the vast hospital property, I had a motorized scooter and a radio to call for assistance. Whenever any situation was uncontrollable, we had the options of calling the local military police from the Naval Base or the Philadelphia police department to assist. The F.B. I. was called whenever we received an anonymous threat against the hospital. We were able to record incoming phone calls including threats made against the hospital. The F.B.I. would come by for the recordings and investigate. Viet Nam was an unpopular war, and there were protest occurring in Washington, D. C. and other areas, including the Na al Hospital in Philly. News media covered the events on a daily basis.

My long-time friend John Stahler spent most of his time off base during non-working hours. He loved to gamble and often lost much more than he won. We would go to the race track in North Philly on occasion and although I would place a bet on a favorite horse, John always played the long shots and ended up losing money. The last time I saw John he had joined Gamblers Anonymous and was trying to cure his gambling habit. My last contact with John was during my third and last tour of duty in Philly during1971. He was a civilian and needed temporary housing for himself and family. I was working at the Metropolitan Hospital in downtown Philadelphia, just across the street from the Police Department.

Metropolitan Hospital Philadelphia-1966

John Stahler and I were the first Navy x-ray techs. To be employed part time at the Metropolitan Hospital. We had heard that the department was losing their night tech that had been working 7 pm til 7am 7 days a week. John and I were interviewed by a fellow named Cummings, Chief Tech for the Radiology Department at the time. After some discussion we agreed that John and I could both cover the shift. We would cover the entire month by splitting the calendar days, working every other night and every other week end. At the end of each month, I would submit a written schedule indicating who was covering the evening shift and each week end. The hourly rate was very good, however there was no shift differential or overtime paid until the hospital unionized a couple of months after we started. As military employees, we were not permitted to join the union, however we did benefit by the pay increases and other changes. There were demonstrations near the hospital during union negotiations, and unfortunately one of the hospital guards was shot and killed. The union was 1199C, very well known on the east coast. On our scheduled shifts, we parked in the hospital parking lot and were escorted to the front door by hospital security guards.

My last memory of working at Metro was the night that the police brought in a teenage boy that was fleeing the police in a stolen car. Apparently his cohort, another teenager, had jumped from the car shortly before the police apprehended the culprits. I was x-raying the kid that was taken into custody, when the police came to the x-ray room to speak to the young man. They informed him that the kid who jumped from the car had been killed and they needed to notify his parents to claim his body. My patient began crying and sobbing, releasing the name and address of the parents. The police thanked him for the information and informed him that his buddy was probably ok, they just needed help in finding him. At the time, the Philadelphia police had a reputation for being aggressive. T-shirts displaying 911-DIAL A BEATING were very popular. I would occasionally hear from my cousin Freddy Schultz who was a police officer (plain clothes) working in North Philadelphia. He had grown a beard and worked with a drug sniffing dog. I lost track of Freddy over the years and often wondered what became of him

Fond Memories of Philadelphia

While living in Philadelphia on my second tour of duty, Bev and I were visited by my father and his wife Tina. They were both living in Brazil Indiana at the time, so it was a full days drive for them. My dad would also visit with my aunts Eleanor and Mildred when he was in town. Both aunts lived in North Philadelphia at the time, with husbands Fred and George plus they each had a son; Freddy (a future Philadelphia police officer), and George who was known for his talent on the piano and organ. During the years that I was stationed in Philly, my aunts and uncles would meet us at the beach near Atlantic City. My uncles would always select a bar that sold clams and beer. We would enjoy a nice lunch and walk the beach. Very nice memories of distant family. Years later, aunt Eleanor had a few health issues, and decided to move to Wapakoneta, Ohio where she lived with my older sister Margaret (Aggie), and she did well living there.

Moving on to Charleston, South Carolina 1968-1973

Charleston Naval Base was the homeport for *USS Robert H. McCard (DD-822)*. The McCard was a Gearing –class destroyer of the United States Navy, named for United States Marine Corps Gunnery Sergeant **Robert H. McCard** (1918-1944), who was posthumously awarded the Medal of Honor for conspicuous gallantry during the battle of Saipan. This would be my last tour of sea duty and one of my fondest memories. The McCard had been in Wes Pac (western pacific) off the coast of Viet Nam. At the end of 1967, McCard transited the Panama Canal and joined the Pacific Fleet. She was now serving on Yankee Station in the Tonkin Gulf. In January and February, she was on plane guard duty for *the USS Coral Sea (CVA-43)* in the Tonkin Gulf, participating in an emergency search and rescue mission on the east cost of Hainan Island.

In March, she served as plane guard for *Kitty Hawk (CVA-63) and Bon Homme Richard* (CVA-31) in the Tonkin Gulf. In April she provided naval gunfire support off South Vietnam, and on May 10th she departed Japan for return to the east coast of the united states. I reported for duty aboard the McCard when she returned to Charleston. My first cruise aboard the McCard occurred in September 1968 when we participated in NATO exercise "Silvertower" in the north Atlantic. Unfortunately, rough weather caused damage to the hull of the ship, requiring repairs, so we put into port at Southhampton, England. It took about one week to make repairs. Most of the crew took advantage of the downtime to take trips to nearby countries. I stayed close to Southampton enjoying the local customs such as fish and chips.

HMC Hunton in Sick Bay

Goosecreek, South Carolina

When Bev and I arrived in Charleston, we checked in at the Naval Base and were informed that government housing on base currently had a waiting list. We then rented a nice brick house in Goose Creek, a short distance from the base. Goose Creek was a very small community and we settled in nicely. A school bus stopped near the house to pick up the girls, and it was short drive to the base. The Charleston area was very scenic and we recognized some of the older houses that had been used in the movie "Gone with the wind." The local water had a sulfur flavor to it, so we got all of our drinking water from town. In a few months we were able to move into Men Riv Park, a fairly new government housing area that was considered very upscale at the time. The new housing area was named for and sponsored by Mendel Rivers, a democratic U.S. Representative from South Carolina representing Charleston-based first congressional district for nearly thirty years. He was a chairman of the House Armed Services Committee as the U.S. escalated its involvement in the Viet Nam war. We lived in a rented house while waiting to get into government quarters.

We had a large back yard that went into a dense wooded area. Unfortunately we often noticed snakes of all varieties in the yard and around our patio enclosure. They liked to lay along the side of our house enjoying the sun, so we were very cautious when allowing our girls go out to play. My next door neighbor was walking through the woods on a sunny day and a large snake was coiled up, blocking his path, he cautiously walked backwards to avoid any confrontation, however after taking two steps, he bumped into an alligator. At this point he simply took off running out of the woods.

From our kitchen window I had a clear view of the wooded area, which was also a swampy area. Since our yard was not fenced in, all types of creatures could enter our yard from the wooded area. One day I started to notice that we were being visited by a pig. Since there was no other homes within my view I assumed it might be a wild pig, and decided to scare him off. I used my 22 caliber rifle to fire a few rounds in his direction. Unfortunately, one of the rounds struck the pig and killed him. I ended up burying him in the wooded area. A week or so later, an old farmer came knocking at our back door looking for a stray pig. I decided to tell him that we had not seen any pigs lately. The weather in Charleston was great for playing golf, even in the winter. My fellow golfers always warned me to take care and carry a golf club with you when looking for a lost golf ball in the "rough area". Snakes seem to be everywhere. When we finally moved in Men Riv Park, we thought our worries about snakes was over, however about two months after moving in, Bev found a cotton mouth water moccasin in our kitchen cabinet wrapped around a wine glass. Next to our phone was a list of numbers to be used in the event any critters made their way into our home. Base pest control responded quickly and removed the intruder from our cabinet. Before leaving he gave us a few tips regarding the habits of certain critters. Apparently during the rainy season, snakes will often make entry through the plumbing in the house. He also took us outside and showed area where snakes liked to lay on hot and sunny days.

MenRiv Housing, Charleston 1968

Cotton mouth water moccasin

Reporting for duty

When I reported aboard the McCard in the summer of 1968, I was an HM1 (E-6). I was replacing Vince Orsak, also an HM1. Vince was looking forward to being discharged from the Navy. Apparently he had not received a promotion to Chief Petty after taking the test. He was now looking forward to choosing another line of work. There was also a corpsman "stryker", someone that was not trained as a corpsman, just fulfilling the duties under the direction of someone like Vince. His name was Jerry and appeared to be a very well trained young man. He was from the south and planned on receiving a discharge in few weeks. Jerry's replacement was an HN named Rick Herfurt. Rick was from Cincinnati, Ohio and was a big fan of Cincinnati Reds baseball. Rick and I served together until I left the ship in 1971. I made a lot of friends in the months following my arrival.

Some of my friend included YN1 "Sox" Hickson. Although he held a very important position in the ships personnel office,(located next to Sick Bay), he had an outrageous sense of humor. His first name was not really Sox. When the McCard was in WesPac, they pulled liberty in various Asian ports, where Sox received his nickname. Story goes that when they were sitting in a restaurant eating, someone noticed that Hixson was not wearing any socks that evening. After that incident, whenever Hixson was seen at a bar or restaurant during liberty, crew members would say in a loud voice "Hixson – show us your sox". Hixson would reply by dropping his trousers to his ankles and say "can you see them now"? Apparently this behavior followed Sox back to the states. Years later while attending the ships reunion I was informed that Sox ended up marrying one of the bar girls that he was seeing. Unfortunately, they had an argument and she shot and killed him.

Shipmates 1968-1971

Living aboard ship for months at a time, 24/7 tends to make the crew like your family. Even though we all had family and friends back home, having a friendly bunch of guys aboard ship made our lives a little easier. The Chief's Quarters were located as far forward as you go on the ship, also known as the bow/bau of the ship. We assumed the rationale for this was that chiefs are usually the most experienced sailors on the ship and were able to deal with the rough ride, especially during stormy weather. My bunk was in the lower area against the steel bulkhead (wall), and I could hear the sound of waves striking the ship. Exiting the berthing area via a small ladder I would go directly into the Chief's mess area (dining area. We had our own galley and our own cook that would prepare our meals each day. Next to the galley we had a shower area with three shower heads. I only used the shower at sea, since my house was just twenty minutes from the ship yard. Underway at sea, all hands were required to take a "Navy Shower". The purpose of a Navy shower is to conserve water. You simply turned the shower on. Quickly got wet, turned off the shower while used the soap, then turned the shower back on to rinse off. Anyone not following this protocol was accused of taking a "Hollywood Shower".

Life aboard ship

I found that all of the Chiefs were easy to get along with as well as all of the crew members, which included approximately 275 men. The crew depended on me for their health and welfare. I held sick call twice a day in my small office with a supply of medications and first aid equipment. I could do routine lab test with my microscope, splint injuries, suture lacerations and confine someone to bedrest if I felt it was necessary. I would also have to submit a report to the executive officer with reason for bedrest. A few months after being aboard I passed the test Chief (E7), and met the other criteria for advancement to Chief Petty Officer. It was my first attempt to take the test, so I felt very happy about the results. We were in port at the time and YN1 Hixson almost knocked the Sick Bay door down to tell me the news. The word spread quickly among the crew and my sick bay was flooded with well wishers.

Chief Chief Petty Officers Initiation

The Navy has a unique tradition of recognizing promotion from E6- to E7 (Chief Petty Officer). When a sailor passes the written test and meets all of the criteria such as having adequate time in the pay grade, and no disciplinary actions, he is given a date for promotion. When you make chief, you change uniforms and wear khakis instead of dungarees, plus you wear dress blues or dress whites in the appropriate seasons.

Charleston Reunion photo

On the day of my initiation the McCard was in her homeport of Charleston, South Carolina. I had been given written instructions to report to the Chief's mess (dining area) at 0700. My prescribed uniform was a mixed bag of different uniforms. This part of the initiation was done privately in the Chief's quarters. In the afternoon I was in full proper uniform and escorted to the Chief's club on the base. As part of a long time tradition, I was to stand trial to see if I was worthy of being a Chief Petty officer.

The chiefs club dining area was set up like a court house. The stage where a band would normally be located was occupied by a long table with several chiefs in attendance. A master chief sat in the center holding a gavel and tried to maintain order among the attendees. Only chiefs were invited to the initiations, and most of them had a head start drinking before the actual ceremony started. There was a total of six candidates for initiation and chiefs from their duty station were also in attendance.

USS McCard

Preparing to get underway

About two weeks after the initiation, we had orders to get under for a Mediterranean cruise. I spent most of my time stocking up on medical supplies, and giving shots to everyone that would be on the cruise. If you were a short timer, due for discharge or transfer, you did not get the shots. The type of shots that I gave were based on the geographical areas that our ship would be traveling into. Rick Herfurt, HN (E3) was immensely helpful with this project. He knew the crew well and joked with everyone to make them feel at ease. Shots were usually scheduled for pay days, and held in the crews dining area (mess hall). If you wanted to get paid, you had to walk through the shot line. We also had a check off list, just in case someone failed to show up. Very few of our crewman ever fainted or became ill while receiving shots, however I always had an emergency kit set up in case we had an incident. I had trained Rick for emergencies that could occur while giving immunizations, particularly if someone went into anaphylactic shock, which is the worse case scenario. Anaphylactic shock is described as an extreme often life threatening allergic reaction to an antigen to which the body has become hypersensitive.

Anaphylactic shock is defined as a condition where your blood pressure suddenly drops and your airway narrows possibly blocking normal breathing. This can lead to serious complications including death. Most sailors are screened for allergies which can be a leading cause for this condition. I have encountered sailors that became dizzy or fainted, however a whiff of ammonia usually brought them around. Anyone with lingering symptoms was sent to the base dispensary to see a doctor. Anyone that was on daily medications was also sent to the dispensary for evaluation.

North Africa

After making all preparations we were on our way across the Atlantic and had great weather all the way across to our destination. Our point of entry would be with Europe on our left (port side) and Morocco (Africa) on our right side (starboard). Shortly after arriving in the Med, I was walking on the main deck early one morning and felt sand blowing in my face. I was informed that there was a storm in Morocco and we could see dust clouds on the horizon. During our time in the Med, the McCard would visit Palma Spain, where six of the chiefs had their picture taken in a local bar and I was included. We made a port visit to Morocco, and a few of us took a short ride on a camel.

Gomila Bar and grill, Palm Spain

Other port visits included Barcelona Spain, Naples Italy (also known as the city of thieves), Monaco France, and Greece. In Monaco we had a change of command ceremony. Our ship's captain, (Brown) was leaving for another command and the crew would miss him. Captain Brown was a former enlisted man and was usually empathetic towards the enlisted crew. Grace Kelly and her son Albert attended the ceremony. This was undoubtedly the high point of the cruise. Most of the bars that we frequented spoke a bit of English and since it was close to Christmas they made us feel at home. Monaco was also known for their casinos, however there where not many gamblers in our crew.

Monaco France Circa 1969

Monaco was one of the wealthiest ports our ship had ever visited. Our ship was anchored out in the harbor and while going into town we would pass an extraordinary number of expensive yachts. Princess Grace Kelly was an American film actress who became Princess of Monaco after marrying Prince Ranier in 1956. She passed away on September 14, 1982.

Heading Home to Charleston

We completed our med. Cruise and headed back to Charleston where I received orders to the U.S. Naval Hospital, Philadelphia, Pa. I still have good memories of the men that I served with aboard the McCard including Chief Willie Wilson, YN1 Sox Hixson, Cook Abe Abernathy, store keeper Craig Bair, Chief Lester Hatfield, HN Rick Herfurt, Chief Charlie Haight, Chief Bill McQuarter, Chief Beeler, and Chief Ripley to name a few. After retiring in 1975, I would attend McCard reunions that are held annually and see some of my former shipmates, plus others that had served aboard in prior years. At my first reunion in Branson Missouri, I was asked to help out by taking the minutes of the annual business meeting. I agreed and enjoyed helping out. My fellow officers for the reunion included John Childs, Vic Tornero, Glen Anderson and Steve Shepherd. I attended reunions the next three years and then retired and let Steve take my position of Yeoman.

Returning to the U.S. Naval Hospital Philadelphia (tour #3)

In the summer of 1971 I reported for duty at the Naval Hospital in Philadelphia. I was now a Chief Petty Officer and would be head of the department. My career had just started when I was here as an HN, then HM3 while in the radiology department. I had traveled the world gaining knowledge and skills that would prepare me for an interesting and rewarding career in the Navy. In addition to being trained as a Medical Corpsman, I had also trained as a Radiologic Technologist, Independent Duty Corpsman (Phys. Assistant), Field Medicine Tech. (Fleet Marine Force), and had also received training in Nuclear, Biological, and Chemical Warfare.

Life in Marlton

Bev and our four daughters Patty, Sue, Linda and Debbie had traveled with us and we now resided in Marlton, New Jersey, I had rented a two story house with a nice back yard in a residential area. My increase in paygrade made allowance for decent housing. It was a twenty minute drive across the Walt Whitman Bridge and my family and I enjoyed life in the suburbs. My father Harry and wife Tina visited us on occasion and dad then introduced me to his brother Nelson and cousin Carole living in the area. Nelson was handicapped and lived alone. Hi daughter was an x-ray tech. and we never met her. Carole, dad's niece was recently divorced when we met her. In later years, we learned that Carole did trapshooting as a hobby and had won a national championship in Vandalia, Ohio. On Occasion, she would come to the house for dinner and play pitch and catch with the girls.

Family photo - Bud, Bev and girls

Viet Nam Era Hospital

The hospital was still receiving patients that were injured in Viet Nam. The ramps leading to and from the main building were used as rehab areas for these patients. Unfortunately, there was still much anti-Viet Nam war sentiment in the public area, including threats that were called in to the hospital on a regular basis. Part of my duties now included hospital security when I was Chief of the day. We patrolled the ramps and made rounds to the end of each ramps, including the enlisted men's club at the end of the east ramp. Occasional fights broke out in the club; if the bartenders could not handle it, security was called. On a rare occasion, the local police were called in. Some of the corpsman serving in Philly had Post Traumatic Stress Disorder (P.T.S.D.) from serving in Viet Nam, however this disorder was not acknowledged until years later. Physical therapy was an important part of rehabilitation for the Viet Nam veterans. Unfortunately, the Viet Nam War was not popular with the public, and some radicals were threatening to bomb the hospital. Unfortunately, the veterans were upset with this scenario and felt threatened while they were recovering from their injuries.

Working with the F.B.I

The F.B.I. was investigating the bomb threats that were called into the hospital. Our phones were set up to trace the incoming calls and we maintained a list of suspicious callers. On my duty days I was the liaison for the F.B.I. when they arrived at the hospital to follow up on phone calls that were actual bomb threats. None of the threats were serious and we never had to evacuate the hospital. Security at the main hospital gate was increased, the guards were now armed, and cars were checked thoroughly to avoid any type of threat. In the future, I would also deal with the F.B.I. while working at Grandview Hospital in Dayton, Ohio. I was the Radiology Department administrator, and my department had been implanting nuclear pacemakers in patients. Unfortunately, the pacemakers contained plutonium, an element that can be used to make nuclear weapons. Unscrupulous people were able to use electronic detectors to locate them in cemeteries, dig them up, and sell them on the black market. My office maintained a list of patients that had a nuclear pacemakers implanted, and I had to periodically insure they were still residing at the recorded location. When the patient could not be contacted, the F.B.I. was notified and a report was filed. Special agents followed up on each case.

Fond Memories of Philadelphia

Working in Radiology from 1971 to 1975 brought back a lot of memories. Several of the people I knew during my last two tours had been discharged from the service. About sixty percent of the folks that I previously knew were in for just one term, usually about four years. The others were in for at least twenty years, and were probably still in on active duty somewhere in the world. Years later I hooked up with Facebook and I was able to make contact with some of them. Some of my R.T. (radiologic technologist) friends were now selling x-ray equipment making nice salaries. Jack, Becker, and Ed Ramsey come to mind as successful salesman. John Stahler had moved out west and then returned to Ohio looking for work. Roy Brooks and Timothy Graham (the only black R.T.'s I had worked with) were still working in Radiology as successful managers.

My time served at the Naval Hospital in Philadelphia was educational, interesting and rewarding. I had interacted with several military and civilian residents in the area, and for that I am very greatful. In 1988 under the *base realignment and closure act* (BRAC), the hospital was scheduled for closure and disposal. All hospital functions were relocated from the complex in 1993 and since that date the buildings were vacant and overseen by a small security force and maintenance staff. The hospital was demolished on June 9th, 2001 at 7:02 am.

Life in Retirement

Several years after retiring from the Navy, I was notified via Facebook that the USS Robert H. McCard (DD-822) was hosting reunions with former shipmates. I joined the website and started attending annual reunions. I did some research on the web and discovered that the USS Rankin (AKA-103), was also hosting annual reunions. Online, I could not find anyone on the current Rankin roster that I knew, so I stayed with the McCard Reunions which were usually held around the same time of year, in the fall. My second reunion was held in Branson, Missouri. Very good town for a reunion, lots of things to see and do. On the first day of the reunion I was having breakfast at the hotel restaurant, when John Childs approached me to assist taking notes at the business meeting. I was a bit surprised since I was new to the organization and had absolutely no idea of what the actual duties were, and what was expected. I showed up for the business meeting where John gave an explanation the former "yeoman" had stepped down and he had asked me to take the position. After a quick vote, I was duly elected

USS Robert H. McCard Reunions

In 2013 I attended my first McCard Reunion in Jacksonville, Florida, followed by the Branson reunion in 2014, then the Virginia Beach reunion in 2015 followed by the Charleston, S. C. reunion in 2016. All were well organized events, and I attended with my wife Beverly. At the time John Childs was the president, Vic Tornero was the treasurer, Cal Pepper was the editor for our quarterly newsletter, and I was the yeoman – keeping the membership roster updated and keeping notes for our meetings. Due to health issues, I was unable to attend many of the later reunions, however feedback from Face Book and our quarterly newsletter indicated that annual attendance numbers continued to be high. Military reunions of all types are very popular and provide old friends an opportunity to reunite and reflect on historical events. Navy reunions appear to be an excellent way to enjoy a few days of vacation while staying at an upscale hotel. Every reunion that I attended was well planned and well attended with an average of approximately eighty to one hundred twenty people in attendance. The shipmate is how we describe the former Navy men that served aboard the ship. Several shipmates brought along a guest such as spouse, or significant other.

2017 McCard Reunion

USS Robert H. McCard (DD-822) 2015 reunion Virginia Beach, VA

Bud and Bev Hunton at the 2015 Reunion

Huntons at the Charleston Naval Base

USS McCard Reunion - Charleston, S.C. 2016   USS McCard Reunion 2013, Jacksonville, Fla.

Statue of Sailor

During my twenty years of service in the Navy, I spent time with family in Ohio. Much of Bev's family and mine lived in St. Marys, Ohio. While home on leave I interacted with several nieces and nephews, including Kevin Jackson. Kevin was always curious about my job in the Navy. Kevin Enlisted in the Navy in 1993 until 1996. He trained as a hospital corpsman and was stationed at the Naval Air Station in Orlando Florida and then the Naval Hospital in Millington Tennessee. After his military service, Kevin completed the Physician Assistant Program at the University of Toledo.

Kevin's son Wyatt joined the Navy in 2013, trained as a hospital corpsman and then was stationed at Camp Pendleton, California. He reenlisted for five years, did a six month tour of duty in Australia, and currently is doing a tour of duty with the 1st Marine Division 2nd Battalion 4 Marines, also known as "The Magnificent Bastards". I have spent a little time talking to Wyatt when he was home on leave and he has done very well. I spoke to him last at his dad's graduation from the P.A. program at the University of Toledo.

Relatives with Military Service

Nephew Kenny Waters was a Marine from 1991-1995. Ken was a corporal serving with Camp Lejeune's 2nd Marine Division at Camp Lejeune, North Carolina. Kenny and Kevin are half brothers, sharing mother Sally Waters. My granddaughter Melissa Olds, joined the U.S. Air Force in September 2018. She resides in Colorado with my daughter Patty Halley. She is currently stationed at the Keesler Air Force Base in Biloxi, Missippi. Melissa's father Ed Halley served for twenty years in the U.S. Air Force. He traveled the globe with his wife Patty and their three children. Son in law Jim Wendling was a Marine Corporal, stationed at Camp Lejeune, North Carolina. Jim is married to our daughter Linda Wendling. Brother in law Lee Rice was an Airman U.S.A.F. From September 10th 1952 until August 11th 1956. He was stationed in Amarillo, Texas and Newfoundland. He worked on various aircraft during his time in the military. Lee was married to my sister Jackie, retired to Florida and passed on November 22nd 2017.

Nephew Ken Waters CPL USMC 1991- 1995

Nephews Kevin and Wyatt Jackson
with aunt Bev and uncle Bud

Melissa Olds grand daughter, U.S.A.F Active duty

James Wendling son in law, Cpl U/S.M.C.

Ed Halley, U.S.A.F. Retired

Brother in Law Lee Rice Airman U.S.A.F

George Makley brother in law
Cpl USMC 1968-1970

Bob Makley
SP2/CPL US Army
1955-1957

Kevin Jackson nephew HM3 USN 1993-1996

Wyatt Jackson grand nephew HM3
(FMF) USN 2013-Actively serving

I left the USS Robert H. McCard in 1971, after serving three years on board. Face Book was not available available at that time, so my only contact with former shipmates was an occasional phone call or Christmas card from them. In February 2004, Mark Zuckerberg launched "The Facebook" as it was originally known; the name taken from sheets of paper distributed to freshman, profiling students and staff. A year after I left the McCard, she was transferred to the Naval Surface Reserve Force (NAVSURFRESFOR) in Tampa, Florida where it served as a Naval Reserve training ship berthed adjacent to Naval Reserve Center Tampa. In this capacity, McCard had a crew of approximately 2/3 active duty Regular Navy and full-time active duty Training and Administration of the Reserve (TAR) officers, chiefs and enlisted sailors, and 1/3 part-time Selected Reserve (SELRES) personnel. For the next seven years, McCard would conduct weekday training and upkeep pier side, followed by weekend underway periods in the Gulf of Mexico and annual extended duration training and operational support cruises in the Gulf of Mexico, the Caribbean and the Western Atlantic.

- In 1975, while returning from Halifax, Nova Scotia she encountered foul weather, incurred a forty degree roll that damaged the ship and subsequently was required to pull into Charleston for repairs. She entered the port with a ten degree lisp.
- In 1978 the McCard was tasked to Shadow a Russian task force that was in Cuba. They went to Key West and and then tracked the Russians back to the Tampa Bay area.
- On January 28th 1980 the USCGC Blackthorn a 180 foot buoy tender sank shortly after a collision with the tanker Capricorn near the Sunshine Skyway Bridge. The Blackhorn lost 23 of its 50 crew members in what is considered the Coast Guard's worse peacetime disaster.
- On Friday May 9th, 1980 at 7:33 A.M., the freighter Summit Venture rammed into the Sunshine Skyway Bridge during a severe storm. The bridge's support pier gave way to the 20,000- ton ship. The pier was destroyed and the roadway above crashed into the waters of Tampa Bay. A Greyhound bus crashed into water along with a number of cars. Thirty five lives were lost on that day. Some of the McCard crew remember this event and recall using the McCard's sonar as part of the recovery operation.
- The USS Robert H. McCard (DD 822) ended her days with the Navy on June 5th 1980 in Tampa, Florida where she was decommissioned and turned over to the Turkish Navy. She was renamed Kilig Ali Pasa, and served with the Turkish Navy until she was again decommissioned in 1998. She was scrapped in the year 2000.

EPILOGUE

My twenty years of military service ended in August 1975. I had traveled the globe crossing the Pacific and Atlantic Oceans, visited the Arctic Ocean, cruised the Mediterranean Sea, and Caribbean sea. I interacted with people from various cultures around the world and found it to be an interesting planet. Although I retired with three college degrees, most of my knowledge was gained from interacting with people from all walks of life. As a college educator, I encouraged my students to be *life long learners* meaning that they should be motivated to pursue knowledge for either personal or professional reasons.

"Some people live an entire lifetime and wonder if they have made a difference in the world. A veteran doesn't have that problem

Ronald Reagan

Kevin and Holly

Bud and Bev with daughters Patty, Sue, Linda and Deb

C. Hight, SH2   W.

Wyatt and family celebrating Kevins Graduation
from University of Toledo P.A. Prog HM2
Hunton at Camp Leujne, N.C.

Current C.O. of the McCard Association

Doug McKay X.O. and wife Cookie

USS Robert H. McCard Reunion 2019

Mr and Mrs John Childs John is former C.O.

Mr. and Mrs. Ron Perceful (Ron is currently the Yeoman)

Hospitality Room at the reunion.

Glen Anderson (Paymaster)

Annual fundraising auction for the McCard Association

Plank Owner Donald Hicks

Mr. and Mrs. Vic Tornero

Printed in the United States
By Bookmasters